MW01489398

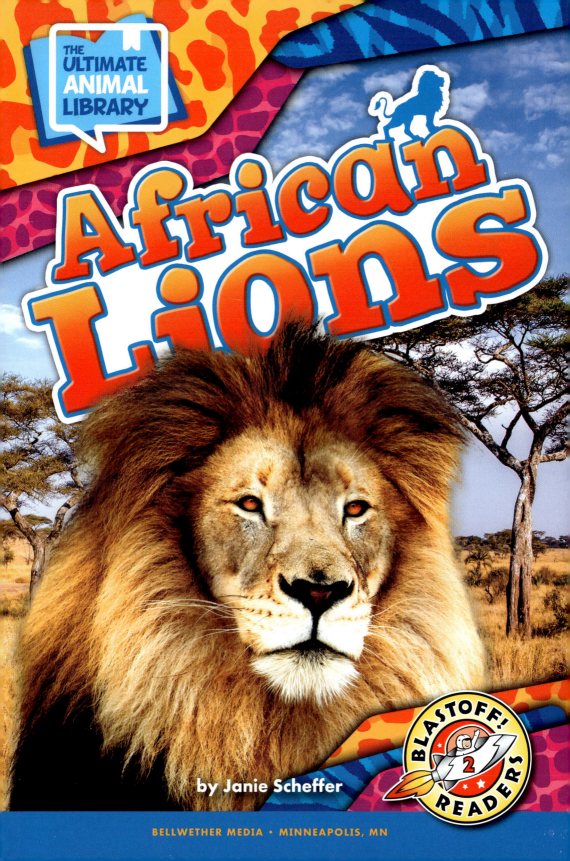

THE ULTIMATE ANIMAL LIBRARY

African Lions

by Janie Scheffer

BELLWETHER MEDIA • MINNEAPOLIS, MN

BLASTOFF! READERS 2

Blastoff! Readers are carefully developed by literacy experts to build reading stamina and move students toward fluency by combining standards-based content with developmentally appropriate text.

Level 1 provides the most support through repetition of high-frequency words, light text, predictable sentence patterns, and strong visual support.

Level 2 offers early readers a bit more challenge through varied sentences, increased text load, and text-supportive special features.

Level 3 advances early-fluent readers toward fluency through increased text load, less reliance on photos, advancing concepts, longer sentences, and more complex special features.

★ **Blastoff! Universe**

Reading Level

Grade **K**

Grades **1–3**

Grade **4**

This edition first published in 2025 by Bellwether Media, Inc.

No part of this publication may be reproduced in whole or in part without written permission of the publisher. For information regarding permission, write to Bellwether Media, Inc., Attention: Permissions Department, 6012 Blue Circle Drive, Minnetonka, MN 55343.

Library of Congress Cataloging-in-Publication Data

LC record for African Lions available at: https://lccn.loc.gov/2024012099

Text copyright © 2025 by Bellwether Media, Inc. BLASTOFF! READERS and associated logos are trademarks and/or registered trademarks of Bellwether Media, Inc. Bellwether Media is a division of Chrysalis Education Group.

Editor: Elizabeth Neuenfeldt   Series Designer: Veah Demmin

Printed in the United States of America, North Mankato, MN.

Table of Contents

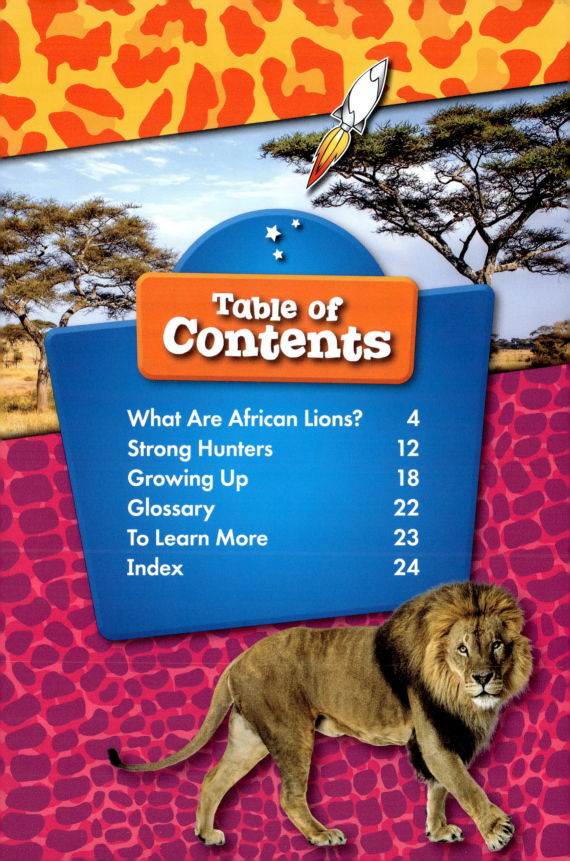

What Are African Lions?

African lions are wild cats. They are the second-biggest cats in the world. These **mammals** live in Africa.

African Lion Report

Range

N
W · E
S

range =

Status in the Wild

▼
✓ ✓ ✓ ✓ ✓ ✓ ✓ ✗
▲
vulnerable

Habitats

grasslands

open
woodlands

savannas

African lions have golden fur. This helps lions blend into tall grass.

female

male

mane

Males have **manes** around their heads. These **protect** their necks from attacks.

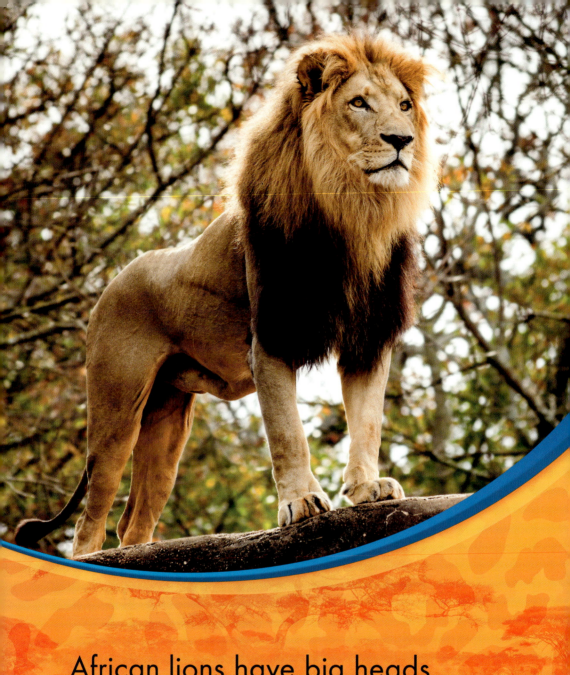

African lions have big heads. Their bodies are long and strong.

 8

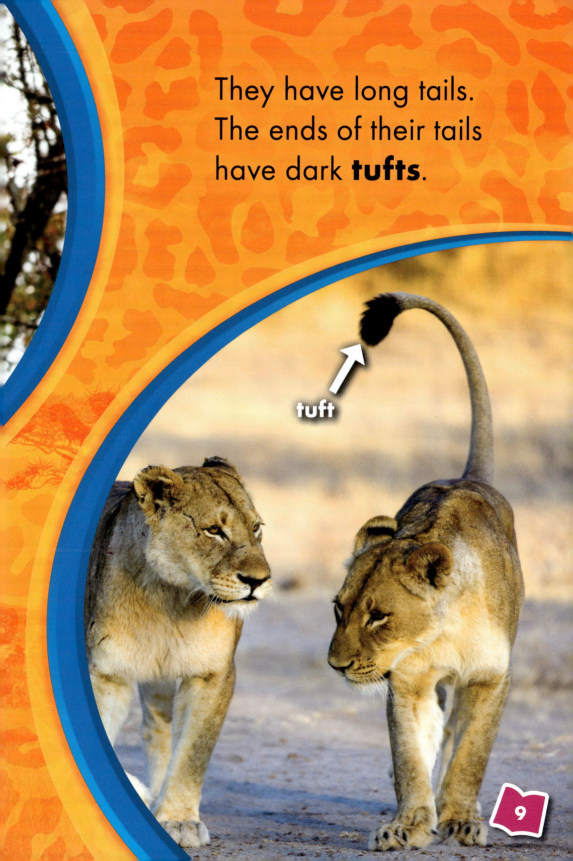

They have long tails.
The ends of their tails
have dark **tufts**.

tuft

African lions have large paws. They have sharp, **retractable** claws.

Lions have sharp teeth. Their strong jaws can open 11 inches (28 centimeters) wide!

paw

Spot an African Lion

golden fur

mane (males)

long body

dark tuft on tail

11

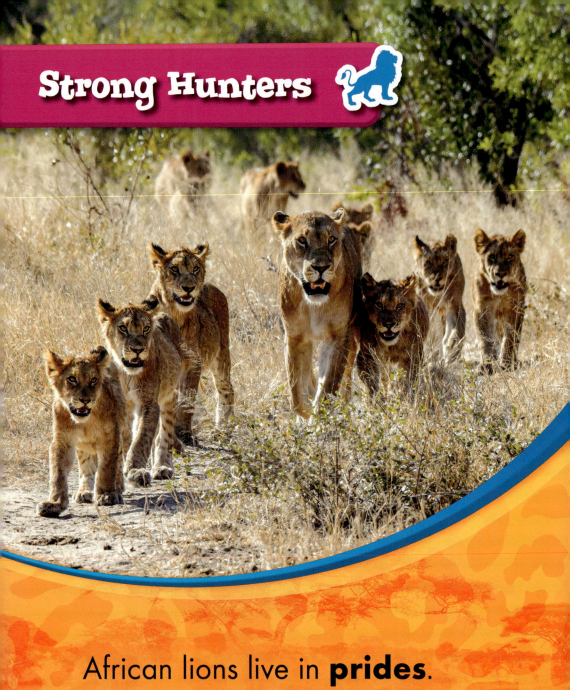

African lions live in **prides**.
A pride has up to 40 lions!

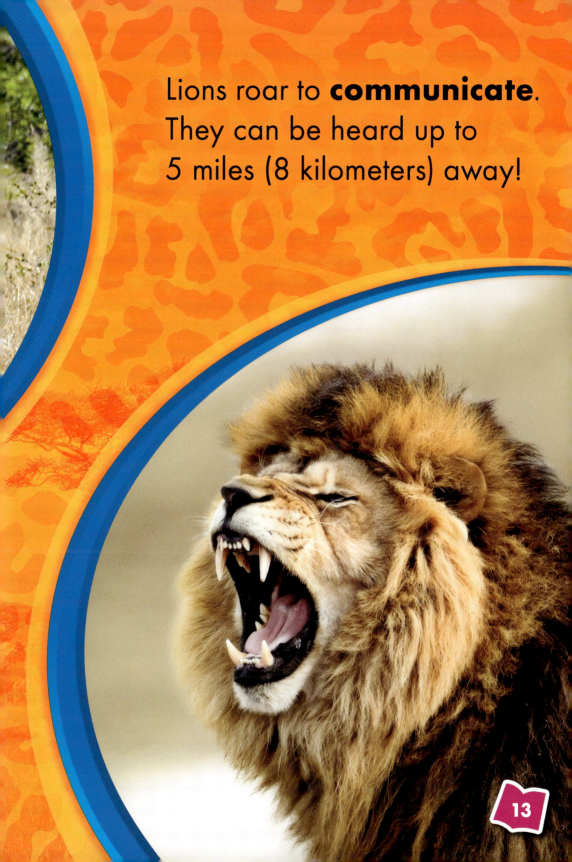

Lions roar to **communicate**. They can be heard up to 5 miles (8 kilometers) away!

13

African lions live in hot **savannas**. They rest under trees to stay cool during the day.

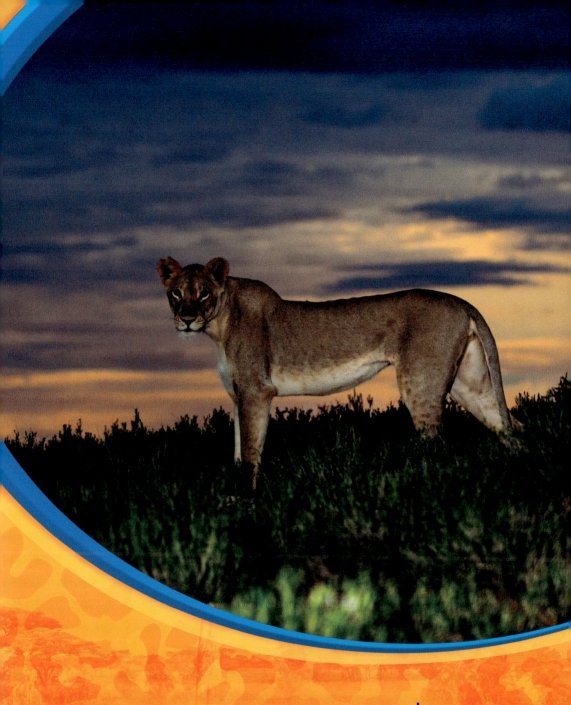

Lions move more at night.
The weather is cooler.

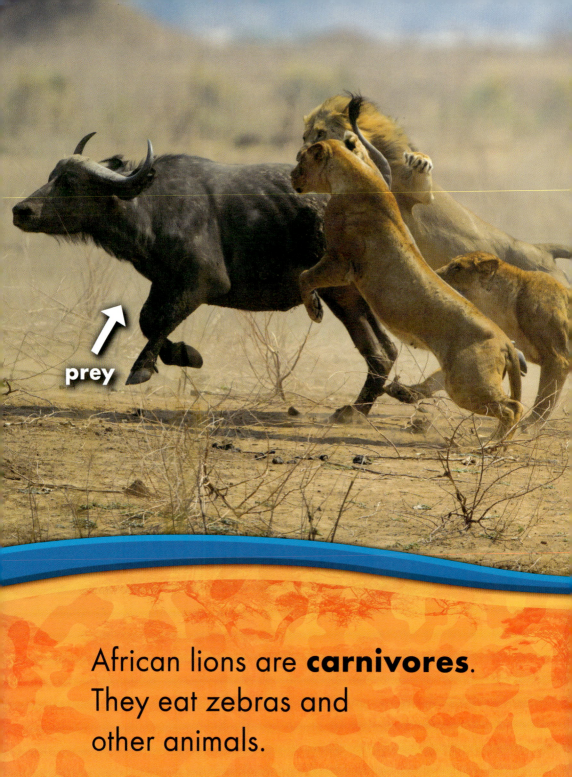

prey

African lions are **carnivores**. They eat zebras and other animals.

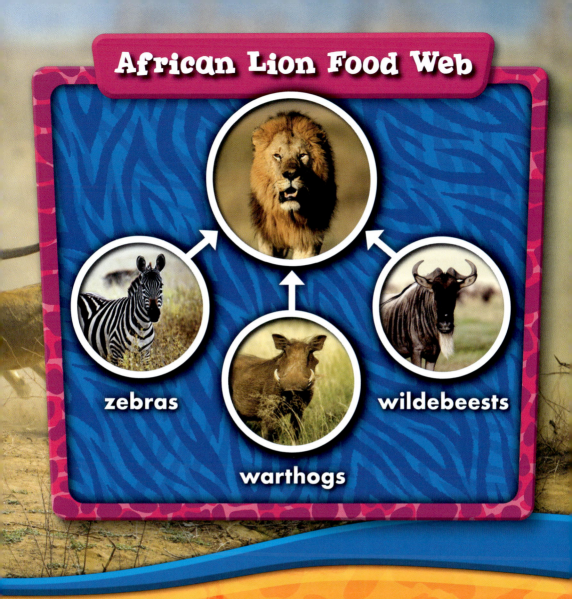

African Lion Food Web

zebras

warthogs

wildebeests

Lions catch **prey** with
their sharp teeth and claws.
Females usually hunt in groups.
Males often hunt alone.

Growing Up

African lion **cubs** are born with spots. Their spots go away as they grow.

Females have up to six cubs in a **litter**. Females in a pride raise cubs together.

cub

litter

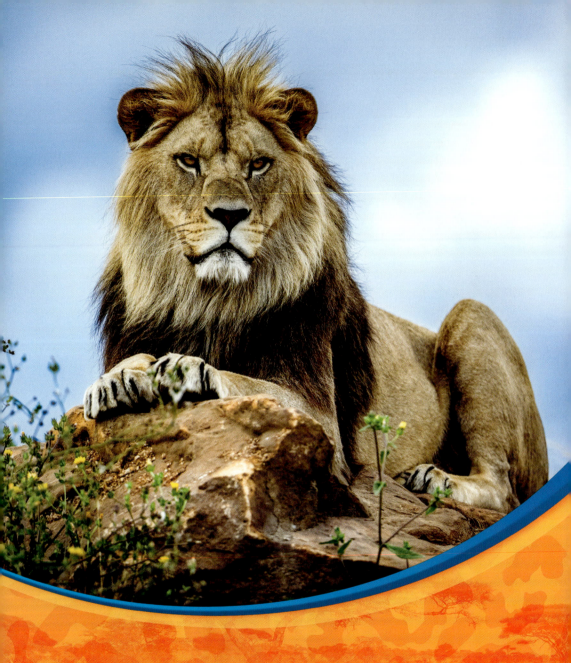

African lions grow up
in two or three years.

Females stay with their pride. Males leave to lead their own pride!

Life of an African Lion

Name of Babies

 cubs

Number of Babies

 up to 6

Time Spent with Mom

 2 or 3 years

Life Span

 up to 18 years

Glossary

carnivores—animals that only eat meat

communicate—to send and receive information

cubs—baby African lions

litter—a group of baby animals born at one time

mammals—warm-blooded animals that have backbones and feed their young milk

manes—shaggy hair around the necks and heads of some animals

prey—animals that are hunted by other animals for food

prides—groups of lions

protect—to keep safe

retractable—able to be pulled back in

savannas—flat grasslands with few trees

tufts—bunches of fur

To Learn More

AT THE LIBRARY

Duling, Kaitlyn. *African Lions*. Minneapolis, Minn.: Bellwether Media, 2020.

Jaycox, Jaclyn. *African Lionesses: Hunters of the Pride*. North Mankato, Minn.: Pebble, 2023.

Riggs, Kate. *Lions*. Mankato, Minn.: Creative Education, 2025.

ON THE WEB

FACTSURFER

Factsurfer.com gives you a safe, fun way to find more information.

1. Go to www.factsurfer.com.

2. Enter "African lions" into the search box and click 🔍.

3. Select your book cover to see a list of related content.

Index

The images in this book are reproduced through the courtesy of: InnaPoka, series patterns; Simon Dannhauer, cover background, interior background; Albertus Bonke, cover (African lion); aditya M S, cover (lion icon); Eric Isselee, pp. 3, 11; PHOTOCREO Michal Bednarek, pp. 4, 17 (zebras); Gerrit_de_Vries, p. 6; ArtMediaFactory, p. 7; Rob Hainer, p. 8; Mark Dumbleton, p. 9; desant7474, p. 10; Volodymyr Burdiak, pp. 10-11; Diana Rebman/Alamy, p. 12; Stepan Kapl, p. 13; Lasse Johansson, p. 14; HANNES LOCKNER, p. 15; Jez Bennett, pp. 16-17; Dr Ajay Kumar Singh, p. 17 (African lion); Arab, p. 17 (warthogs); Papa Bravo, p. 17 (wildebeests); Keith Kenkinson, p. 18 (inset); pjmalsbury, pp. 18-19; AB Photographie, p. 20; Sue Green, p. 21; Dennis Jacobsen, p. 23.